*Luke Chapter 2, verses 1 to 20*

*Illustrations copyright* © 1982 Nord-Süd Verlag, Mönchaltorf & Hamburg

An Abelard/North-South Book
*First published in Great Britain 1982 by*
Abelard-Schuman Ltd
*A Member of the Blackie Group*
Furnival House, 14-18 High Holborn, London WC1V 6BX

British Library Cataloguing in Publication Data
 The Christmas story.
  1. Jesus Christ–Nativity–Juvenile literature
  2. Bible (Texts, versions, etc.)
  I. Watts, Bernadette
  II. Die Weihnachtsgeschichte. *English*
  226'.4'05203        BS2593

 ISBN 0-200-72791-5

*Printed in Belgium*

# THE CHRISTMAS STORY

*with pictures by Bernadette Watts*

Abelard/North-South

And it came to pass in those days, that there went out a decree from Caesar Augustus, that all the world should be taxed.

And all went to be taxed, every one into his own city.

*And Joseph also went up from Galilee, out of the city of Nazareth, into Judea, unto the city of David, which is called Bethlehem; (because he was of the house and lineage of David:) To be taxed with Mary his espoused wife, being great with child.*

And so it was, that, while they were there, the days were accomplished that she should be delivered.

And she brought forth her first-born son, and wrapped him in swaddling clothes, and laid him in a manger; because there was no room for them in the inn.

And there were in the same country shepherds abiding in the field, keeping watch over their flock by night.

And, lo, the angel of the Lord came upon them, and the glory of the Lord shone round about them: and they were sore afraid.

And the angel said unto them, "Fear not: for, behold, I bring you good tidings of great joy, which shall be to all people.

"For unto you is born this day in the city of David a Saviour, which is Christ the Lord.

*"And this shall be a sign unto you; Ye shall find the babe wrapped in swaddling clothes, lying in a manger."*

And suddenly there was with the angel a multitude of the heavenly host praising God,
and saying,

"Glory to God in the highest, and on earth peace, good will toward men."

And it came to pass, as the angels were gone away from them into heaven, the shepherds said one to another, "Let us now go even unto Bethlehem, and see this thing which is come to pass, which the Lord hath made known unto us."

*And they came with haste, and found Mary, and Joseph, and the babe lying in a manger.*

*And when they had seen it, they made known abroad the saying which was told them concerning this child.*

*And all they that heard it wondered at those things which were told them by the shepherds.*

*But Mary kept all these things, and pondered them in her heart.*

*And the shepherds returned, glorifying and praising God for all the things that they had heard and seen, as it was told unto them.*